Shades of LOVE

LGBTQ+ Coloring Book

Inspiring Designs with Affirming Messages of Love and Acceptance

by
Ronald Holt and
William Huggett

Copyright © Ronald Holt and William Huggett, 2018

All rights reserved. No part of this book may be reproduced in any form without permission in writing from the authors. Reviewers may quote brief passages in reviews.

Published 2018

ISBN 13: 978-0-9985829-9-3

DISCLAIMER: No part of this publication may be reproduced or transmitted in any form or by any means, mechanical or electronic, including photocopying or recording, or by any information storage and retrieval system, or transmitted by email without permission in writing from the authors.

The authors do not assume any responsibility for errors, omissions, or contrary interpretations of the subject matter herein. Any perceived slight of any individual or organization is purely unintentional.

The contents of this book are provided for informational purposes only, and should not be used to replace the specialized training and professional judgment of a licensed health care or mental health care professional. The authors cannot be held responsible for the use of information provided. This book does not constitute the formation of a physician–patient relationship. Please always consult a physician or trained mental health professional for personal issues.

Self-help information and information from this book are useful, but are not meant to be a substitute for professional advice.

Are you a member of the LGBTQ+ communities? Or do you know someone who is? Many people in these communities are forced to deal with discrimination and rejection. Shades of Love LGBTQ+ Coloring Book offers messages of hope and inspiration with beautifully drawn mandala designs.

Coloring is a way to bring peace and focus. The designs provide a framework for reflection and growth.

Shades of Love LGBTQ+ Coloring Book includes 30 beautifully drawn designs, each with an affirmation. This book embraces and celebrates the diversity of love.

We are diverse communities. We believe strength and healing come when we embrace diversity. So we welcome everyone with messages of love, hope, and inspiration.

As you go into the stillness of coloring, we encourage you to enter into whatever process allows your deeper self to emerge. We invite you to grow and expand into the beautiful, authentic person that only you can be.

You are worthy of unconditional love and acceptance – just the way you are.

To get more information about Dr. Holt, his speaking engagements, other books or videos, please visit DrRonHolt.com. You can find more information about Dr. Huggett at WilliamHuggett.com.

Sincerely-

Love is blind
and knows no gender.

Love is love is love.

Loving myself as I am allows everything else to fall into place.

No matter where I am in my journey,
I am loved.

There are many people
who love and support me.

I am not alone.

No matter how I identify,
my love is valid.

The butterflies I feel
come from love, not fear.

True love is always unconditional.

True love is unconditional

All love deserves equality.

My first and last love will always be self-love.

Love should never need to hide.

I love myself wholeheartedly.

I love myself wholeheartedly

My greatest gift: Loving myself.

Love is real.
Period.

I give and receive unconditional love.

I cherish being loved
just as I am.

I am worthy of unconditional
love and acceptance.

Love trumps hate.

Love is to be celebrated.
Not diminished.

Every day I take time to experience
the love that connects us all.

No one determines who I love
or how I love.

My love is mine to give,
so I give it away freely.

We must stand strong
and support one another.

You may be facing challenges right now.
But I believe in you.
I love you.

Love is better when embraced in all it's forms.

I love being me.

I choose to surround myself
with those who love me for me.

Love begins with accepting myself.

Indeed.
Without a doubt.
Love is unequivocal.

True love sets us free.

www.ingramcontent.com/pod-product-compliance
Lightning Source LLC
Chambersburg PA
CBHW081021040426
42444CB00014B/3308